GOD MADE THE WORLD

This is a story about God making a beautiful world with everything in it. He made it for you and He made it for me!

THIS STORY begins so long, long ago, that only God and the Angels can remember when it happened. God the Father said to God the Son and God the Holy Spirit, "Let's make some people. They can take the place of the bad angels, and be happy with Us forever in Heaven." So God, the Blessed Trinity, set out to make some people. But first, the people would need a world to live in. So God made the world.

AT FIRST everything was all dark and empty. God said, "Let there be light!" And all at once there was light. God called the light "day." The darkness He called "night." That was the first day in the world–Number 1 on the calendar!

ON THE SECOND DAY, God said, "Let there be sky," and there it was. God made it out of nothing at all.

On the third day, God said, "Let the water come together in one place, and let the dry land come out." So that is what happened. What do you think God called the dry land? He called it "earth." And the place where the water was all together, running and splashing, He called "seas."

THEN GOD MADE plants grow on the earth. He made grass and trees and all kinds of flowers. When this was finished, God looked it all over and saw that it was good. Everything was green and fresh and beautiful. But something else was needed.

SO ON THE FOURTH DAY, God made the sun, to shine during the day.

AND THEN GOD made the moon, to shine at night. The sun and the moon would tell the days and the months.

THIS WAS STILL the fourth day, and God was still making things. He made many, many lights and called them "stars." They are really very big lights, but they are so far away that they look little to us. God's world is so very big! His stars shining at night are so very beautiful! The next time you see the stars, say quietly inside, "Thank You, God!" God likes us to appreciate the beautiful things He made for us. He likes to hear us say thank you for them, too!

how would you play IF you had no toys or games or books?

Once when I was little, I tripped over a rug and broke my thumb. At first I didn't know it was broken. I ran to my parents, who were having tea in the garden, and called: "See how funny my thumb looks: it's all crooked!" My parents didn't think it funny at all. They put me in the car and drove me to the doctor.

When the doctor put on a plaster cast, it didn't just go up to my wrist, it didn't just reach my elbow, either—it went *way up* almost to my shoulder and was to stay on for several weeks. It was my right hand, too!

For a while it was fun, trying to do everything with one hand and training to be a "south paw." But after a while it wasn't fun any more, and I was bored, too, because I was left out of so many games my friends played.

Trying to think of something new to do, I wandered through the house and looked at everything there. Of course, I had seen everything before, but as I looked at the things now, I tried to give them names, like people. I looked at them very carefully to see if they reminded me of anyone I knew. Then I named them after whomever it was.

There was a brown pot with a lid like a hat. Mother used it for our cocoa. It reminded me of a neighbor who loved to wear brown dresses, so I called it *Mrs. Finchley.* I called the tea kettle *Uncle Charles,* because when Uncle Charles smoked his pipe, he blew clouds just like the kettle when the water was boiling. A dark, straight chair looked like *Mr. Spencer,* who always sat up straight as an arrow when he came to visit us. *Minnie* was the mop, after a friend of mine who had very unruly hair. Then there was *Grandpa,* the easy chair, and *Aunt Eleanor,* the tea cozy with the flowers all over it, and many others.

I told only my sisters about it and we kept it a secret among ourselves. For a while we surprised the grown-ups with remarks like this: "You have been sitting on *Grandpa* all afternoon! It's my turn now, you sit on *Mr. Spencer.*" Or, "Where is *Minnie? Mrs. Finchley* spilled her cocoa." And, "I can't find *Aunt Eleanor* and I know I put her in the top drawer this morning!"

Of course, it is a very silly game—I guess that is why it is so much fun!

CLOTHESPIN PEOPLE

You need somebody who can handle a saw and will help you to saw short the *legs* of some clothespins. Then you need some paint or crayons and some good glue. You might also look around for a small piece of heavy cardboard or a piece of thin wood, like the bottom of a cheese box, before you start on your clothespin people.

Mrs. Clothespin has short legs. She gets a skirt and a blouse, and perhaps an apron—all painted on, of course! Be sure you remember the face and arms while you are painting.

Mr. Clothespin has longer legs. They are his trouser-legs. He can have coat-tails in the back and a bow-tie in front. He could wear a glued-on toothpaste cap for a hat. He and his wife may have painted hair or a glued-on wig of feathers, thread or unravelled string.

You can make all kinds of different people, like a father going on a walk with his twins, Peg and Peggy. Or a teacher with a class of children.

To make your little people stand up, you simply glue them onto the piece of cardboard, which you can paint like a meadow full of flowers or like a carpet. You must also paint the shoes of the people who will be standing on it. To get the feet of your funny friends glued into the right position, trace around the feet, then put the glue in those spots.

SICK AND TIRED

There was a little man
and he lay in his bed
with a bump on his nose
and a hole in his head,
with the measles and mumps,
with a fever and chills,
and the doctor prescribed him
some medicine and pills.

When the little man got better
he still stayed in bed,
with no bump on his nose,
with no hole in his head,
with no measles or mumps
without fever or chills,
without medicine to take
and without any pills.

Now I think that perhaps
you may wonder like me:
just what kind of a crazy
little man can he be?
If he now is all well,
he should get up quick.
But he's so sick and tired
—of being sick!

ROSEMARY'S SECRET FRIEND

Rosemary had a secret friend who could not walk, who could not talk, who was not even really alive, but who was the best listener in the world. When other people were too busy or too tired to listen, this friend was never too busy or too tired. You see, this secret friend was her doll!

At night in bed Rosemary would have felt lonely if her doll had not been with her. Until she fell asleep, she talked to her about everything that was on her mind.

In the mornings it was her doll who got the first hug, even before her parents. Her doll was included in everything.

"Now I can't take you with me today," she would say on a busy day, "because Mother and I are going out. You stay right here, and don't feel lonely. I will tell you about everything tonight."

But you must not think that everybody could hear the things the little girl told her doll. Oh no! She only talked to her in her heart, not with loud words. As I told you before, it was a *secret* friend!

Of course, her parents knew that she loved her doll. They could see that the toy was getting worn from use, and most of the paint had been kissed off its face. Therefore, one Christmas, they planned to have the doll repaired and re-painted by an artist, as a special present for their little daughter.

So it happened that a few days before Christmas, Rosemary could not find her doll. She looked everywhere for her little friend. There were ever so many things she wanted to talk about, especially before Christmas! She missed her terribly. But when she asked her parents if they had seen her doll, they only smiled mysteriously and said:

"Wait until Christmas. Who knows what is going to happen!"

Then Rosemary guessed that Christmas must have something to do with her lost doll, and she did not search for her any longer.

At last Christmas came. As soon as the family came home from church, they went into the living room, which had been locked for several days.

That year Rosemary had no eyes for the Christmas tree or any of the presents. She was looking for her doll. But the minute she saw her, all the joy went out of her heart. It was not her friend! Her friend had had dark brown hair and brown eyes. The doll before her had small blue eyes, and the painted hair was light brown. She looked at Rosemary as if she had never seen her before. She looked as if she had never understood a word of all the things Rosemary had told her. And yet, by the patches on the knees and the tilt of the head, Rosemary could tell that it was her old doll.

Rosemary's parents did not understand why their little girl burst into tears. And all she could say between sobs was:

"I wish Christmas had never come!"

How could she explain that the artist's paint had killed her secret friend?

Maybe her Mother did understand a little about her sadness. She took her for a walk, and when they passed the church, she said:

"Let's go inside and visit the Christ Child."

While they knelt before the Christ Child in the manger, Rosemary's mother told her about the first Christmas, how there had been no room for God when He was born as a Child so many winters ago, and that He had had to lie in a hard manger.

"It was God's own Son," she said, "who came down to earth, to show people how much He loved them. But the people had no room for Him."

Rosemary looked at the beautiful Child. Her heart grew warm inside her.

"I would have made room for Him," she thought. "He is so small. He would even fit in my doll's bed."

Suddenly she was thinking of her lost friend again. And again she looked at the Child Jesus.

"Who takes care of Him when He isn't here any longer, after Christmas?" she asked her mother hopefully.

Her mother gave her a quick kiss.

"This is just a doll, darling, like yours," she said, "which does not need to be cared for. It is only here to remind us of the *real* Christ Child.

"You know, it is sometimes hard to love and remember somebody we have never seen. We think of the real Christ Child when we look at this little doll in the crib scene. When we see the picture of the poor stable, we remember that the real Christ Child has been born and is looking for room in our hearts. We can keep Him warm there, if we love Him enough."

"Can He be in many hearts at the same time?" asked Rosemary.

"Yes. Remember, He was not always the little Baby Jesus. He grew up and became Our Saviour Jesus Christ, who died for us on the Cross. But because He was God, He rose again from the dead and went back to Heaven. Like God the Father, He can be everywhere. He can live in every heart. He is always with us, as long as we try to be close to Him."

Rosemary looked again at the little wax baby. Then she closed her eyes and tried to think of the real Christ Child. Her heart grew warm with love as she imagined Him so small and cold in the dark night. She talked to Him in her heart, as she used to talk to her doll.

When she opened her eyes again, she saw the crucifix above the altar.

"Did He look like that when He was a man?" she asked.

"Not exactly, darling. This crucifix was made by an artist, like all the statues in this church. We love them because they tell us of God and His Saints, and their great love, so that we may learn to love them too."

Rosemary was very quiet on their way home. Her heart felt happy and light inside her. This had been a *real* Christmas, because she had made room in her heart for the Infant Jesus.

Not only for Christmastime had she promised to keep Him there, but all through the year. Even when there was no Christmas crib to remind her.

At night, her mother noticed that Rosemary did not take her doll to bed with her as she used to do. Instead, she carefully tucked her into the doll's bed and said:

"Don't worry. I'll still play with you. You can't help it that you are only a doll and all changed, and I'm not sad about it any longer, because now I have a secret friend who is *real* and never changes."

From that day on, besides the prayers she said with her mother, Rosemary always talked to Jesus in her heart with her own words. As soon as she woke up, she remembered that He was there. She told Him that she loved Him and that she would not forget Him during the day, even when she was busy with other things.

At bedtime, she told Him about everything that had happened during the day. When she had done something wrong, she told Him about it, and she told Him how sorry she was. Rosemary knew that He felt and saw everything that went on in her heart, because He lived there. She also knew that He would understand that she could not always be good. It made her feel very safe to know that He loved her much more than she could ever love Him, and that He would teach her to do the right things as she grew older.

During the day too, Rosemary often talked to her new secret friend. Whenever something sad happened to her or other people, she asked Him to make it right. And when something made her happy, she told Him:

"Thank You, Jesus. And help me to say Thank You to God, because You are His Son."